For my little loves, Jamie and Molly,
whose smiles and silliness are constant
reminders of Jesus' love for me.

Published by Concordia Publishing House

3558 S. Jefferson Avenue, St. Louis, MO 63118-3968

1-800-325-3040 • www.cph.org

Text © 2017 by Jonathan Schkade

Illustrations © 2017 by Concordia Publishing House

Manufactured in Heshan, China/047365/300655

1 2 3 4 5 6 7 8 9 10   26 25 24 23 22 21 20 19 18 17

The Love Bridge
LEARNING ABOUT JESUS

Jonathan Schkade • Illustrated by Tim Bradford

CONCORDIA PUBLISHING HOUSE • SAINT LOUIS

God loves you!

God loves everyone.

God created the world
for the people He loves.

Sins are our bad thoughts, words, and choices.

We are born sinful.

When we sin, brokenness spreads.

Our sin broke the road between us and God.

Still, God reached out to us in love.

God sent His Son, Jesus,
to fix this brokenness.

Jesus showed love to everyone.

He fed and healed many people, and He brought God's Word to us all.

He knew how broken we were, so He took all our sins on Himself.

Then He carried those
sins to the cross.

Jesus died.

But on the third day, on Easter, He came alive again.

Jesus is the love bridge to God. He is our way to God.

Our loving God sends
His Spirit to us.

The Spirit gives us faith
to believe that Jesus
died to forgive our sins.

God heals our brokenness with Jesus' love and forgiveness.

God gives us love in many ways now.

And someday God will take us across the bridge of Jesus' love to live with Him forever in heaven.

I am the way, and the truth, and the life. No one comes to the Father except through Me.

John 14:6

AUTHOR

Jonathan Schkade (rhymes with "body") is a procrastinator, pardoned sinner, and freelance author. In addition to *Icky Sticky, Hairy Scary Bible Stories* and the Not-So-Nice Bible Stories series, he's a regular contributor to the Arch Book® series, *My Devotions*®, and *Portals of Prayer*®.

Jonathan lives with his wife, Kristi, and their lovely, lovable daughters in Jefferson City, Missouri. He sings in the men's choir at Immanuel Lutheran Church in Honey Creek, Missouri, and spends his free nanoseconds reading, cooking, going to movies, and trying not to be too much of a nuisance.

ILLUSTRATOR

Tim Bradford is an illustrator and animator living right next to a nature reserve in Nottingham, United Kingdom, and also has the convenience of being just half a mile from the city center. From alpine landscapes to geometry to animals, he is inspired by nature and loves drawing people of all sizes, shapes, and nationalities.